CW01464972

Twelve Poems
for Christmas

Twelve Poems
for Christmas

Selected by Amy Wack

SEREN

Seren is the book imprint of
Poetry Wales Press Ltd.
57 Nolton Street, Bridgend, Wales, CF31 3AE

www.serenbooks.com
facebook.com/SerenBooks
twitter@SerenBooks

Poems © Individual Authors, 2017

The rights of the above mentioned to be identified as
the authors of this work has been asserted in accordance
with the Copyright, Designs and Patents Act, 1988.

ISBN: 978-1-78172-467-5

A CIP record for this title is available from the British Library.

All rights reserved. No part of this publication may be reproduced,
stored in a retrieval system, or transmitted at any time or by any means,
electronic, mechanical, photocopying, recording or otherwise without
the prior permission of the copyright holder.

The publisher acknowledges the financial assistance of the Welsh Books Council.

Cover image: manipulated from 'Reindeers by night' © Jeremy Segrott (CC BY 2.0)

Printed in Bembo by Berforts Ltd, Hastings.

Contents

St Leonore and the Robin

Winter is the long dream
between harvests
when the sea-worn land is sere:

time to remember ploughing
the darkening days,
far from home with no crop to sow

till a robin came with an ear of wheat
shared gladly with him
whose palm warmed her shivering.

Small beginnings prosper
Blessings, gold flame and heart's red,
be upon you.

Pippa Little

St Leonore was a sixth century Welsh missionary to Brittany. After preparing for sowing he
found there was no corn – then a robin came with an ear of wheat which became a golden
field by the next summer. The phrase in italics is a Breton saying, drawn from this story.

Camel

The camel waits on folded knees,
watches from the flat roof that juts

into the yard behind the end of terrace
built from pale yellow London brick

smudged with dust and grime, stray
smuts of soot; the half-lidded gaze

taking in the passers by who saunter
in summer sun, clutch coats close

in winter chill; buses, cars weave
ribboned lights along the city street

and yet, despite the never-ending
traffic fumes, the nostrils flare;

the trappings are spotless, neat
and fringed, the head and hump

gleam, all are gilded as though lit
by a blaze of sun; maybe, indoors,

a time-slip Magi searches Google
Sky, looking for that star, that birth.

Helen Overell

Noticing Cards While Eating Stuffing

The family is trapped in the Victorian coach-and-four,
forever caught whip-whisking over the snow.
The mountain hare will never taste that bright berry;
she's permanently frozen in the act of reaching for it.
The robin, beak open like a shy kid who can't ask
for a date, will never sing, nest or mate.

We're not quite motionless round the dinner table.
The odd hat rustles, the odd fork clinks like a coin
in an empty collecting-tin. It's a stop-motion animation
of Xmas dinner.

One exception: the granddaughter, Laura, whose head
spins and eyes make magic of the heavy meal.
Every cracker yielded treasure; every hoary old film
was fresh. Soon, while the rest of us drift like snow
into heaps of unconsciousness, she will make whole
worlds out of toys not yet broken.

Cathy Bryant

Offering

for Rufus

After the wrapping, unwrapping.
After unwrapping, the mess.
Through paper wasteland my boy wades;
his hot, sticky hands embrace my face,
pressed like a prayer, gargoyling my smile.
Our brown eyes speak of love.

Along with the giving, the learning.
After the learning, his deed.
Up fairylit stairs he charges, inspired;
above me the ceiling clunks like a factory;
he delivers two papers beneath the tree:
one for his daddy, one for me.

After the folding, the hiding, the finding,
the moment of moment: his hurried gifts.
Each scarecrow portrait, carefully drawn,
guards a faded five pound note.
I accept this gold with kisses.
Later I post the paper money back into his box.

Alexandra Davis

What Wish

What wish if not this wish?

That snow is terrible
only in its fall;
that overnight
the sky will clear
and leave the altered earth
unhurt.
That in some warm
neglected stall,
new life can grow;
that winter's sleep
will stir to birth,
rouse shepherds,
frankincense and myrrh,
speak words
to startle Herods,
sear the dark.

What wish if not this wish?

What hope?

Will Johnson

Gabriel's Greeting

It's tough on self-esteem, being the Angel of the Lord.
A herald of good tidings would be met with open arms,
or so you might imagine, but terror is the usual response.
Hence my well-worn default prologue, 'Do not be afraid.'

I'd banked on rather better from the baptizer's father-to-be,
a priest, no less, and isn't the temple the place to expect me.
Apparently not. In the circs, leaving him dumbstruck seemed
fair exchange for his craven need of 'Do not be afraid.'

Then there was the girl. Who anticipates a seven-foot seraph
manifesting over the washing, let alone with the gravid news
that turns kid into Theotokos? A quick-draw reassurance
seemed the least I could do. I meant it, 'Do not be afraid.'

And her young man – one of the good guys, a real keeper –
he had my sympathy too. How does a chap get his head,
his heart, round a divine cuckolding, and still have the guts
to do the decent thing? I told him straight, 'Do not be afraid.'

The Night itself, when the guys and I arrived, glory blazing,
sheep and dogs all got the message. Those dozy shepherds
thought they'd been smoking something far more awesome
than the usual mix. Get a grip there, lads, 'Do not be afraid.'

Nowadays this gospel harbinger gets overlooked, by people
too preoccupied to spot what really matters – that scares me.
Beyond life's mess, if they had eyes to see and ears to hear,
the Boss's Xmas, all-year, Word remains, 'Do not be afraid.'

Sarah Rowland Jones

A Child for Our World

Christus natus hodie
     owls and angels sing it
     bats and belfries ring it
hang the holly, bind the bay
     let mistletoe revive the kisses
     that our darkened world is missing.

Christus natus hodie
     to lift a child from the sea
     to shield a child from the sky
to guide a child on his way
     fill his belly, fuel his spark –
     to lighten every grieving heart.

Gina Wilson

On Losing my Voice at Christmas

Obviously, loss of   is due to an infection,
probably a seasonal gift from some spluttering
fellow commuter, viruses having multiplied
through a mild December. For such things
there is no magic cure. I must just wait
for my immune system to kick-in. Truth
to tell, loss of   doesn't really affect
my festive roles of chief present handler,
sous-chef to a son, orchestrator, placator
and general factotum. I croak and whisper
at my children, all back to be with Mum
and cracking jokes at the coincidence
of my lack of   and their home-coming.

Nancy Charley

Two Pheasants

Waking to white ground – my brain, cold and slow
said snow. Just frost. A coppery light held
the tops of trees and fields until
                                    two pheasants appeared
from nowhere (they always appear from nowhere) –
paused,
looked up, and the low, rising sun lit their chests
burnishing them to copper shields.
                                    Heads down again,
gingerly inching forward, steely pedestrians
but gleaming, like two of the Three Kings;
a secret *rete mirabile* saving their bare feet
        bone and sinew,
unlike my nerves turned to ice picks, climbing the walls
of fingers and toes.
                      They single-filed out of view –
where to?
              Do they always have a plan?

              In the heavy heart of winter, a gift:
two pheasants. Frost. Copper light. I don't think
there's anything in summer to compare to this.

Nicola Healey

*Rete mirabile: Latin for 'wonderful net'. A fine, netlike pattern of arteries and veins
that helps to keep birds' feet from freezing.*

Daylight is in Short Supply

We are connoisseurs
of darkness.
We are able
when we wake
in the night
to judge the hour
precisely
by the shade of black.
From the first stars
to the darkest hour,
to the long stretch of dawn –
trust me.
And three o'clock darkness
is a particularly purple dark.
A darkness
which smells of Rome
and Roman villas.
A darkness
which is a mosaic
of black tiles
squinted at from a distance –
its shape and pattern
make some sort
of sense that way.
It is good
to leave the house
before sunrise
and follow the track
north-east by east.
Your gravelly footsteps
and the warmth
of your body
as your body warms up.
It is good to feel part
of something

you don't comprehend.
It is good to talk
to the blackbird
and the wren.
The mountain streams
are gushing
with yesterday's downpours.
The sound of a car
is the wind in the trees.

Philip Rush

Guardians

Who are they, the ones
who walk with us
over the fields, across the streets,
those who guide us through this?

Fine gardeners, they tend
to selves in cities, schools and farms;
toting babies, coffee, stories,
sharing bread and milk and songs.

We see them every day
brushing coal dust from their arms
or plaiting a child's hair,
reaching into high corners with feathers.

Never far from grace,
they burn like the evening star
guiding us with something
close to love.

Sarah Westcott

The Usual Suspects

Fezzes and Fedoras and the dying strains
of 'Away in a Manger'

and you wonder at yourself watching it again
on Christmas Day, revelling in

'As Time Goes by', instead of 'Silent Night':
the famous: *Play it Sam*,

the landing lights, the last glass of champagne,
the tears in Ilsa/Ingrid's eyes,

the relief of knowing how it will end:
the same every time.

Wendy Klein

The Poets

'St Leonore and the Robin'
Pippa Little's second full collection *Twist* came out in March 2017 from Arc. She lives in Northumberland and is a Royal Literary Fund Fellow at Newcastle University.

'Camel'
Helen Overell lives in the Mole Valley and has published widely in magazines and anthologies. Her first collection is *Inscapes & Horizons* (St Albert's Press, 2008) and her second is *Thumbprints* (Oversteps Books, 2015). Her website is: www.overell.co.uk

'Noticing Cards While Eating Stuffing'
Cathy Bryant's books are: *Contains Strong Language and Scenes of a Sexual Nature, Look at All the Women*, and *How to Win Writing Competitions*. She has won 27 writing competitions and literary awards. Cathy also runs the Comps and Calls site, listing free opportunities for impoverished writers. www.compsandcalls.com/wp

'Offering'
Alexandra Davis lives in Suffolk with her husband and four sons and teaches English. Her first pamphlet, *Sprouts*, was recently published after winning the Brian Dempsey Memorial Prize 2017. Her website is at www.alexandrapoet.wordpress.com.

'What Wish'
Will Johnson lives in Cardiff. His publications include poems in *Poetry Wales, The SHOp, Agenda, Magma, Poetry Salzburg Review, Live Canon 2017 Anthology*, and a pamphlet, *My Speaking Tongue* (Eyewear, 2017). He has also published six India-related books (as W.J. Johnson), including two verse translations from the Sanskrit.

'Gabriel's Greeting'
Sarah Rowland Jones is a priest in the Church in Wales, whose poetry has appeared online and in anthologies in the UK and in South Africa where she spent a decade. Before ordination she was a mathematician, and then a diplomat.

'A Child for Our World'
Gina Wilson's second pamphlet, *It Was and It Wasn't* (Mariscat Press), was published in September, 2017. Her first, *Scissors, Paper, Stone* (HappenStance Press) appeared in 2010. She is also the author of novels and poetry for young adults and children (Faber, Cape, Walker Books). She is a psychotherapist in Oxford.

'On Losing my Voice at Christmas'
Nancy Charley is the Archivist for the Royal Asiatic Society, London. *This Woman*, was published by Conversation Paperpress in 2012, and *Little Blue Hut* by Smokestack Books in 2017. She lives in Kent and spends her free time in London and the south-east indulging in poetry-telling.

'Two Pheasants'
Nicola Healey's poems have appeared in *The Poetry Review* and *The Dark Horse*. She was commended in the Hippocrates Prize for Poetry and Medicine 2017, and in the Resurgence Poetry Prize 2015. Her book *Dorothy Wordsworth and Hartley Coleridge: The Poetics of Relationship* was published by Palgrave Macmillan in 2012.

'Daylight is in Short Supply'
Philip Rush lives in a Stroud cottage. He runs Yew Tree Press, a small, pamphlet press for local and other poets. His poems have appeared in UK and US magazines and in Carcanet and Bloodaxe anthologies. He teaches English, runs workshops and plays Irish fiddle music on a French violin.

'Guardians'
Sarah Westcott's first collection, *Slant Light*, was published in 2016 by Pavilion Poetry and a poem from it was Highly Commended in the Forward Prizes. She grew up in north Devon and lives in Kent with her family.

'The Usual Suspects'
Born in New York, **Wendy Klein** left the U.S. in 1964. A retired psychotherapist, she has spent most of her adult life in England. She has two collections from Cinnamon Press: *Cuba in the Blood* (2009), *Anything in Turquoise* (2013) and a third, *Mood Indigo*, from Oversteps Books.

SEREN

Well chosen words

Seren is an independent publisher with a wide-ranging list which includes poetry, fiction, biography, art, translation, criticism and history. Many of our books and authors have been on longlists and shortlists for – or won – major literary prizes, among them the Costa Award, the Jerwood Fiction Uncovered Prize, the Man Booker, the Desmond Elliott Prize, The Writers' Guild Award, Forward Prize and TS Eliot Prize.

At the heart of our list is a beautiful poem, a good story told well or an idea or history presented interestingly or provocatively. We're international in authorship and readership though our roots are here in Wales (Seren means Star in Welsh), where we prove that writers from a small country with an intricate culture have a worldwide relevance.

Our aim is to publish work of the highest literary and artistic merit that also succeeds commercially in a competitive, fast changing environment. You can help us achieve this goal by reading more of our books – available from all good bookshops and increasingly as e-books. You can also buy them at 20% discount from our website, and get monthly updates about forthcoming titles, readings, launches and other news about Seren and the authors we publish.

www.serenbooks.com